The World's Greatest Collection of Clean Jokes

Bob Phillips

HARVEST HOUSE PUBLISHERS
EUGENE, OREGON

Cover by Dugan Design Group, Bloomington, Minnesota

THE WORLD'S GREATEST COLLECTION OF CLEAN JOKES
Copyright © 1998 by Bob Phillips
Published 2013 by Harvest House Publishers
Eugene, Oregon 97402
www.harvesthousepublishers.com

ISBN: 978-0-7369-4848-7 (pbk.)
ISBN: 978-0-7369-4850-0 (eBook)

Printed in the United States of America

13 14 15 16 17 18 19 / BP / 10 9 8 7 6 5 4 3 2 1

Contents

Introduction

As one attempts to write a book, even a joke book, he often encounters periods of depression and a slowing of motivation. During periods of depression, I was spurred on by an important quote designed for writers:

> If you steal from one author, it's plagiarism;
> If you steal from two or three authors, it's literary discernment;
> If you steal from many, it's masterful research.

Joke telling can be a lot of fun. Or it can be a disaster, like the man who told a joke and everyone booed except one man—he was applauding the booing.

If you would like to guarantee disaster in your joke telling, follow these suggestions:

1. Make sure you forget the punch line; sadists enjoy a letdown.

2. Laugh at your own joke and be sure to jab your audience during the process.

3. Tell the same story over if the point is missed. This will assure at least wry smiles.

4. Make sure the story is long enough to lull the dull ones to sleep.

5. Tell the wrong joke to the wrong audience; they'll feel worse than you do.

6. Above all else, don't be yourself because you know you're not humorous, even if you are funny.

If, on the other hand, you would like to have some measure of success in joke telling—ignore these suggestions.

—Bob Phillips

Adam and Eve

At what time of day was Adam born?
A little before Eve.

When was radio first mentioned in the Bible?
*When the Lord took a rib from Adam and made a
    loudspeaker.*

Eve: Adam, do you love me?
Adam: Who else?

Adam and Eve were naming the animals of
the earth when along came a rhinoceros.

"What shall we call this one?" Adam asked.
"Let's call it a rhinoceros," said Eve.
"Why?" responded Adam.
"Well, it looks more like a rhinoceros than anything we've named yet!" Eve replied.

Teacher: Why was Adam a famous runner?
Student: Because he was first in the human race.

Adam was created first . . . to give him a chance to say something.

What a good thing Adam had—when he said something he knew nobody had said it before.

The first Adam-splitting gave us Eve, a force which men in all ages have never gotten under control.

Airplanes

Passenger: Excuse me. How high is this plane?
Flight Attendant: About 30,000 feet.
Passenger: And how wide is it?

The loudspeaker of the big jet clicked on and the captain's voice announced in a clear, even tone: "Now there's no cause for alarm but we felt you should know that for the last three hours we've been flying without the benefit of radio, compass, radar, or navigational beam due to the breakdown of certain key components. This means that we are, in the broad sense of the word, lost and not quite sure in which direction we are heading. I'm sure you'll be glad to know however, that we're making excellent time!"

10

An airliner flew into a violent thunderstorm and was soon swaying and bumping in the sky. One very nervous lady happened to be sitting next to a clergyman and turned to him for comfort.

"Can't you do something?" she demanded.

"I'm sorry, ma'am," said the reverend gently. "I'm in sales, not management."

A man is now able to go across the United States in eight hours . . . four hours for flying, and the other four to get to the airport.

❖ ❖ ❖

The airline company was disturbed over a high percentage of accidents and decided to eliminate human errors by building a completely mechanical plane.

"Ladies and gentlemen," came a voice over a loudspeaker on the plane's maiden voyage, "it may interest you to know that you are now traveling in the world's first completely automated plane. Now just sit back and relax because nothing can possibly go wrong . . . go wrong . . . go wrong . . . go wrong . . ."

That airplane flight was so rough that the flight attendants poured the food directly into the sick sacks!

Pilot: Control tower, what time is it?
Control tower: What airline is this?
Pilot: What difference does that make?
Control tower: If it is United Airlines, it is 6:00 P.M.; if it is TWA, it is 1800 hours; if it is Smogarian Air, the big hand is on the . . ."

Passenger: Say, this is the worst steak I've ever had. Don't you flight attendants even know how to serve a steak? Bring me another steak right now!
Flight attendant: Will that be to take out?

Flight attendant: I am sorry, Mr. Jones, but we left your wife behind in Chicago.
Man: Thank goodness! I thought I was going deaf!

Pilot: Pilot to tower . . . pilot to tower . . . I am 300 miles from land . . . 600 feet high and running out of gas . . . please instruct . . . over.

Tower: Tower to pilot. . . . tower to pilot . . .
repeat after me . . . "Our Father, which art in
heaven . . ."

The other day one of those jumbo jets took
off from New York with 400 passengers, then
had to make a forced landing in Newark
because of a hernia.

Last week I was flying on a plane and almost
had a heart attack when I noticed a sign on the
door of the pilot's cabin that said "Student
Pilot."

3

Army and Police

Officer: Soldier, do you have change for a dollar?
Soldier: Sure, buddy.
Officer: That's no way to address an officer.
   Now, let's try that again. Soldier, do you have
   change for a dollar?
Soldier: No, sir!

An Army base staff that was planning war
games didn't want to use live ammunition.
Instead they informed the soldiers: "In place of a
rifle, you go, 'Bang, bang.' In place of a knife,
you go, 'Stab, stab.' In place of a hand grenade,
you go, 'Lob, lob.'"

The game was in progress when one of the
soldiers saw one of the enemy. He said, "Bang,
bang," but nothing happened. He ran forward
and shouted, "Stab, stab," but nothing

happened. He ran back and went, "Lob, lob," but nothing happened. Finally he walked up to the enemy and said, "You're not playing fair. I went 'Bang, bang' and 'Stab, stab' and 'Lob, lob' and you haven't fallen dead yet!"

The enemy responded, "Rumble, rumble, I'm a tank."

A very new soldier was on sentry duty at the main gate of a military outpost. His orders were clear: No car was to enter unless it had a special sticker on the windshield. A big Army car drove up with a general seated in the back.

The sentry said, "Halt, who goes there?"

The chauffeur, a corporal, said, "General Wheeler."

"I'm sorry, I can't let you through. You've got to have a sticker on the windshield."

The general said, "Drive on."

The sentry said, "Hold it. You really can't come through. I have orders to shoot if you try driving in without a sticker."

The general repeated, "I'm telling you, son, drive on."

The sentry walked up to the rear window and said, "General, I'm new at this. Do I shoot you or the driver?"

A blowhard Air Force major was promoted to colonel and received a brand-new office. His first morning behind the desk, an airman knocked on the door and asked to speak to him. The colonel told him to come in. Then, feeling the urge to impress the young airman, the major picked up his phone and said: "Yes, General, thank you. Yes, I will pass that along to the president this afternoon. Yes, goodbye, sir."

Then turning to airman he barked, "And what do you want?"

"Nothing important, sir," said the airman. "I just came to install your telephone."

❖ ❖ ❖

Just before a farm boy had his first parachute jump, his sergeant reminded him, "Count to ten then pull the first rip cord. If it snarls, pull the second rip cord for the auxiliary chute. After you land, our truck will pick you up."

The paratrooper took a deep breath and jumped. He counted to ten and pulled the first cord. Nothing happened. He pulled the second cord. Again, nothing happened. As he careened crazily earthward, he said to himself, *I'll bet that truck won't be there either!*

One day a sergeant came into the barracks and asked his men if any of them knew shorthand. The recruits thought it would be easy duty and raised their hands.

"Good," said the sergeant. "They're shorthanded in the mess hall!"

Bill: My wife just got a ticket for speeding.
Ray: That's nothing! My wife is so bad the police gave her a season ticket.

A driver tucked this note under the windshield wiper of his automobile: "I've circled the block for 20 minutes. I'm late for an appointment, and if I don't park here I'll lose my job. 'Forgive us our trespasses.' "

When he came back he found a parking ticket and this note: "I've circled the block for 20 years, and if I don't give you a ticket, I'll lose my job. 'Lead us not into temptation.'"

❖ ❖ ❖

The car stalled at a traffic light as the lights went from red, to green, to yellow, to red, to green, to yellow, to red. Finally a cop came up and asked, "Pardon me, sir, but don't we have any color you like?"

"Hello, police department? I've lost my cat and . . ."

"Sorry, sir, that's not a job for the police, we're too busy."

"But you don't understand . . . this is a very intelligent cat. He's almost human. He can practically talk."

"Well, you'd better hang up, sir. He may be trying to phone you right now."

"What am I supposed to do with this?" grumbled the motorist as the police clerk handed him a receipt for his traffic fine.

"Keep it," the clerk advised. "When you get four of them, you get a bicycle."

Things are so bad in our town that the police department has an unlisted telephone number.

The best safety device is a rearview mirror with a cop in it.

Officer to a man pacing the sidewalk at 3:00 A.M.:
     What are you doing here?
Gentleman: I forgot my key, officer, and I'm
     waiting for my children to come home and
     let me in.

A rookie officer was asked the following
question on his examination paper: "How would
you go about dispersing a crowd?"

He answered: "Take up an offering. That
does it every time."

Game warden: Fishing?
Man without a license: No, drowning worms.

❖ ❖ ❖

Stranger: Catch any fish?
Fisherman: Did I! I took 30 out of this stream
     this morning.
Stranger: Do you know who I am? I'm the
     game warden.
Fisherman: Do you know who I am? I'm
     the biggest liar in the country.

Judge: Order in this court! I'll have order in
    this court!
Man: I'll have a hamburger with onions!

In the traffic court of a large Midwestern city,
a young lady was brought before the judge to
answer for a ticket given her for driving through
a red light. She explained to his honor that she
was a schoolteacher and requested an immediate
disposal of her case so she could get to the
school on time. A wild gleam came into the
judge's eye.

"You're a schoolteacher, eh?" said he.
"Madam, I shall realize my lifelong ambition.
I've waited years to have a schoolteacher in this
court. Sit down at that table and write 'I went
through a red light' 500 times!"

Burglar: The police are coming! Quick, jump out
    the window!
Accomplice: But we're on the thirteenth floor!
Burglar: This is not the time to be superstitious.

The other day a guy pointed a gun at me
and said, "Stick 'em up and congratulations!"

I asked, "What's the congratulations for?"

He said, "You are now entering a lower tax bracket."

A bank robber held up a bank. "Give me all your money," he demanded.

"Here, take the books, too. I'm short 10,000 dollars," replied the teller.

"Excuse me for being nervous," the sheriff apologized as he slipped the noose over the condemned man's head. "This is my first hanging."

"Mine too!" replied the criminal.

A fellow walked up to me and said, "Stick 'em down."

I said, "You mean stick 'em up?"

He said, "No wonder I haven't made any money."

A young soldier, an officer, a little old lady, and an attractive young woman were riding on a train.

Shortly after the train entered a dark tunnel, the passengers heard a kiss, then a loud slap.

The young woman thought: "Isn't that odd, the officer tried to kiss the old lady and not me?"

The old lady thought: "That is a good girl with fine morals."

The officer thought: "That soldier is a smart fellow; he steals a kiss and I get slapped."

The soldier thought: "Perfect. I kiss the back of my hand, clout an officer, and get away with it."

A burglar entered the house of a Quaker and proceeded to rob it. The Quaker heard noises, took his shotgun downstairs, and found the burglar. He aimed his gun and said gently: "Friend, I mean thee no harm, but thou standest where I am about to shoot."

An FBI agent was talking to a bank teller after the bank was robbed for the third time by the same bandit.

"Did you notice anything special about the man?" he asked.

"Yes, he seems better dressed each time," the teller replied.

Bald

If a man is bald in front, he's a thinker. If he's bald in the back, he's a lover. If he's bald in front and back, he thinks he's a lover.

"Papa, are you growing taller all the time?"
"No, my child. Why do you ask?"
" 'Cause the top of your head is poking up through your hair."

A bald man's retort: "In the beginning God created all men bald. Later He became ashamed of some and covered them with hair."

He has wavy hair—it's waving goodbye.

He's not bald . . . he just has flesh-colored hair.

He's a man of polish . . . mostly around his head.

There's one proverb that really depresses him: "Hair today, gone tomorrow."

He has less hair to comb, but more face to wash.

It's not that he's bald . . . he just has a tall face.

There's one thing about baldness . . . it's neat.

There's a new remedy on the market for baldness. It's made of alum and persimmon juice. It doesn't grow hair, but it shrinks your head to fit what hair you have.

5

Barbers

I couldn't stand my boy's long hair any longer, so I dragged him with me and ordered, "Give him a crew cut." The barber did just that, and so help me, I found I'd been bringing up somebody else's son!

I've got a 16-year-old son who was 6' 3" until he got a haircut. Now he is 5' 8".

The customer settled himself and let the barber put the towel around him. Then he told the barber, "Before we start, I know the weather's awful. I don't care who wins the next big fight, and I don't bet on the horse races. I know I'm getting thin on top, but I don't mind. Now get on with it."

"Well, sir, if you don't mind," said the barber, "I'll be able to concentrate better if you don't talk so much!"

A man entered a barber shop and said, "I am tired of looking like everyone else! I want a change! Part my hair from ear to ear!"

"Are you sure?"

"Yes!" said the man.

The barber did as he was told and a satisfied customer left the shop.

Three hours passed and the man reentered the shop. "Put it back the way it was," he said.

"What's the matter?" asked the barber. "Are you tired of being a nonconformist already?"

"No," he replied, "I'm tired of people whispering in my nose!"

Customer (twice nicked by the barber's razor): Hey, barber, gimme a glass of water.
Barber: What's wrong, sir? Hair in your mouth?
Customer: No, I want to see if my neck leaks.

Bible Quiz

When were automobiles first mentioned in the Bible?
When Elijah went up on high.

What simple affliction brought about the death of Samson?
Fallen arches.

Who was the most successful physician in the Bible?
Job. He had the most patients.

Who was the best financier in the Bible?
Noah. He floated his stock while the whole world was in liquidation.

Who is the straightest man in the Bible?
Joseph. Pharaoh made a ruler out of him.

Where is tennis mentioned in the Bible?
When Joseph served in Pharaoh's court.

What animal took the most baggage into the ark?
The elephant. He took his trunk, while the fox and the rooster only took a brush and comb.

What man in the Bible had no parents?
Joshua, the son of Nun.

Who is the smallest man in the Bible?
Some people believe that it was Zacchaeus. Others believe it was Nehemiah (Ne-high-miah), or Bildad, the Shuhite (Shoe-height). But in reality it was Peter, the disciple. He slept on his watch!

When is baseball mentioned in the Bible?
When Rebecca walked to the well with the pitcher, and when the prodigal son made a home run.

When is money first mentioned in the Bible?
When the dove brought the green back to the ark.

Who is the most popular actor in the Bible?
Samson. He brought the house down.

Do you know how you can tell that David was older than Goliath?
Because David rocked Goliath to sleep!

What instructions did Noah give his sons about fishing off the ark?
Go easy on the bait, boys. I only have two worms.

Joe: Was there any money on Noah's ark?
Moe: Yes. The duck took a bill, the frog took a green back, and the skunk took a scent.

Why didn't they play cards on Noah's ark?
Because Noah sat on the deck.

How did Jonah feel when the great fish swallowed him?
Down in the mouth.

When is high finance first mentioned in the
    Bible?
*When Pharaoh's daughter took a little prophet from
    the bulrushes.*

When did Moses sleep with five people in one
    bed?
When he slept with his forefathers.

Teacher: Where was Solomon's temple?
Student: On the side of his head.

Fay: How long did Cain hate his brother?
Ray: As long as he was Abel.

Boys and Girls

"When I went out with Fred, I had to slap his face five times."

"Was he that fresh?"

"No! I thought he was dead!"

Girl: Did you kiss me when the lights were out?
Boy: No!
Girl: It must have been that fellow over there!
Boy, starting to get up: I'll teach him a thing or two!
Girl: You couldn't teach him a thing!

You can't kiss a girl unexpectedly . . . only sooner than she thought you would.

"Well, and how are you getting on with your courtship of the banker's daughter?"

"Not so bad. I'm getting some encouragement now."

"Really, is she beginning to smile sweetly at you or something?"

"Not exactly but last night she told me she'd said 'no' for the last time."

On a lonely, moonlit country road the engine coughed and the car came to a halt.

"That's funny," said the young man. "I wonder what that knocking was?"

"Well, I can tell you one thing for sure," the girl answered icily. "It wasn't opportunity."

Boy: Why won't you marry me? Is there someone else?
Girl: There must be.

"I just had a date with Siamese twins."
"Did you have a good time?"
"Yes and no."

Girl: The man I marry must be as brave as a
    lion, but not forward; as handsome as Apollo,
    but not conceited; as wise as Solomon, but
    meek as a lamb; a man who is kind to every
    woman, but loves only me.
Boy: How lucky we met!

"Without you, everything is dark and
dreary. . . . The clouds gather and the wind beats
the rain . . . then comes the warm sun. . . . You
are like a rainbow."

"Is this a proposal or a weather report?"

Joe: What's so unusual about your girlfriend?
Moe: She chews on her nails.
Joe: Lots of girls chew on their nails.
Moe: Their toenails?

"Why does my sweetheart always close her
eyes when I kiss her?"

"Look in the mirror and you'll know."

John: You must marry me. I love you; there can
    be no one other . . .

Mary: But, John, I don't love you . . . you must
find some other woman . . . some beautiful
woman . . .
John: But I don't want a beautiful woman . . . I
want you.

Boy: You know, sweetheart, since I met you, I
can't eat . . . I can't sleep . . . I can't drink.
Girl: Why not?
Boy: I'm broke.

"My girlfriend takes advantage of me."
"What do you mean?"
"I invited her out to dinner, and she asked
me if she could bring a date!"

After a blind date a fellow mentioned to his
friend: "After I got home last night, I felt a lump
in my throat."
"You really like her, huh?"
"No, she's a karate expert."

Girl: Will you marry me?
Boy: No, but I'll always admire your good taste.

34

"Do you have the book *Man, Master of Women*?" a young man asked the librarian.

"Fiction counter to your left," the librarian replied.

Boy, with one hand cupped over the other: If you can guess what I have in my hand, I'll take you out tonight.
Girl: An elephant!
Boy: Nope! But that's close enough. I'll pick you up at 7:30.

A schoolboy took home a library book whose cover read *How to Hug*, only to discover that it was volume seven of an encyclopedia!

Boy: Ah, look at the cow and the calf rubbing noses in the pasture. That sight makes me want to do the same.
Girl: Well, go ahead . . . it's your cow.

Girl: Do you think you could be happy with a girl like me?
Boy: Perhaps . . . if she isn't too much like you.

"How come you go steady with Eloise?"
"She's different from other girls."
"How so?"
"She's the only girl who will go with me."

He: Oh, my dear, how can I leave you?
She: By train, plane, or taxi!

Boy: Gladys, do you love me?
Girl: Yeah.
Boy: Would you be willing to live on my
income?
Girl: Yes, if you'll get another for yourself.

Girl: I'm telling you for the last time—you can't
kiss me!
Boy: I knew you would weaken!

Girl: Do you love me?
Boy: Yes, dear.
Girl: Would you die for me?
Boy: No . . . mine is an undying love.

John: Don't you think I'm rather good looking?
Judy: In a way.
John: What kind of way?
Judy: Away off.

Bill: That girl in the red dress isn't very smart.
Phil: I know. She hasn't paid any attention to me
either.

She: Look at my engagement ring.
Chi-Chi: That's a lovely ring. It's nice to know
you're not marrying a spendthrift.

Boy: Boy, if I had a nickel for every girl I've
kissed . . .
Girl: You'd be able to buy a pack of gum!

Cannibals

My uncle is a cannibal. He's been living on us for 20 years.

First cannibal: We've just captured a movie star.
Second cannibal: Great! I was hoping for a good ham sandwich.

Then there's the missionary the cannibal couldn't boil. He was a friar.

Cannibal cook: Shall I stew both of these Navy cooks?
Cannibal king: No. One's enough. Too many cooks spoil the broth.

❖ ❖ ❖

A resourceful missionary fell into the hands of a band of cannibals.

"Going to eat me, I take it," said the missionary. "You wouldn't like me." He took out his pocketknife, sliced a piece from the calf of his leg, and handed it to the chief. "Try it and see for yourself," he urged.

The chief took one bite, grunted, and spat.

The missionary remained on the island 50 years. He had a cork leg.

9

Church, Preachers, and Sunday School

Reverend Henry Ward Beecher entered Plymouth Church one Sunday and found several letters awaiting him. He opened one and found it contained the single word, "Fool."

Quietly and with becoming seriousness he shared the letter with the congregation and announced: "I have known many an instance of a person writing a letter and forgetting to sign his name, but this is the only instance I have ever known of someone signing his name and forgetting to write the letter."

Did you hear about the church janitor who also played the piano on Sunday? He watched his keys and pews.

❖ ❖ ❖

Did you hear about the country parson who decided to buy himself a horse? The dealer assured him that the one he selected was a perfect choice.

"This here horse," he said, "has lived all his life in a religious atmosphere. So remember that he'll never start if you order 'Giddy-up.' You've got to say, 'Praise the Lord.' Likewise, a 'Whoa' will never make him stop. You've got to say, 'Amen.' "

Thus forewarned, the parson paid for the horse, mounted him, and with a cheery "Praise the Lord" sent him cantering off in the direction of his parish. Suddenly he noticed that the road ahead had been washed out, leaving a chasm 200 yards deep.

In a panic, he forgot his instructions and cried "Whoa" in vain several times. The horse just cantered on. At the very last moment he remembered to cry "Amen" . . . and the horse stopped just short of the brink of the chasm. But alas! That's when the parson, out of force of habit, murmured fervently, "Praise the Lord!"

A conscientious minister decided to get acquainted with a new family in his congregation and called on them one spring evening.

After his knock on the door, a lilting voice from within called out, "Is that you, Angel?"

"No," replied the minister, "but I'm from the same department."

A young businessman returned home after a tough day at the office and found his two daughters, both about kindergarten age, acting up pretty boisterously. He scolded them and sent them off to bed. The next morning he found a note stuck on his bedroom door: "Be good to your children, and they will be good to you. God."

Did you hear the one about the ministers who formed a bowling team? They called themselves the Holy Rollers.

A preacher was called upon to substitute for the regular minister, who had failed to reach the church because he was delayed in a snowstorm. The speaker began by explaining the meaning of a substitute. "If you break a window," he said, "and then place cardboard there instead, that is a substitute."

After the sermon, a woman who had listened intently shook hands with him and, wishing to

compliment him, said, "You were no substitute
. . . you were a real pane!"

The sermon went on and on and on in the
heat of the church. At last the minister paused
and asked, "What more, my friends, can I say?"

In the back of the church a voice offered
earnestly: "Amen!"

Little Jane, whose grandmother was visiting
her family, was going to bed when her mother
called, "Don't forget to include Grandma in your
prayers tonight—that God should bless her and
let her live to be very, very old."

"Oh, she's old enough," replied Jane. "I'd
rather pray that God would make her young."

A minister wound up the services one morning by saying, "Next Sunday I am going to
preach on the subject of liars. And in this con-
nection, as a preparation for my discourse, I
should like you all to read the seventeenth chapter of Mark."

On the following Sunday, the preacher rose
to begin and said, "Now, then, all of you who
have done as requested and read Mark 17,
please raise your hands."

Nearly every hand in the congregation went up.

Then said the preacher, "You are the people I want to talk to. There is no seventeenth chapter of Mark!"

Why are there so few men with whiskers in heaven?

Because most men get in by a close shave.

Little Susie, a six-year-old, complained, "Mother, I've got a stomachache."

"That's because your stomach is empty," the mother replied. "You would feel better if you had something in it."

That afternoon the minister visited and, in conversation, remarked he had been suffering all day with a severe headache.

Susie perked up. "That's because it's empty," she said. "You'd feel better if you had something in it."

"Why do you keep reading your Bible all day long?" a youngster demanded of his grandfather.

"Well," he explained, "you might say I am cramming for my final examinations."

A minister spoke to a deacon and said, "I'm told you went to the ball game instead of church this morning."

"That's a lie," said the deacon, "and here's the fish to prove it."

A hat was passed around the church congregation for an offering for the visiting minister.

Presently it was returned to him . . . conspicuously and embarrassingly empty. Slowly and deliberately the parson inverted the hat and shook it meaningfully. Then raising his eyes to heaven, he exclaimed fervently, "I thank thee, dear Lord, that I got my hat back from this congregation."

✧ ✧ ✧

Hoping to develop his son's character, a father once gave him a penny and a quarter as he was leaving for Sunday school. "Now, Bill, you put whichever one you want in the offering plate," he said.

When the boy returned, his father asked which coin he had given. Bill answered, "Well, just before they sent around the plate the preacher said 'The Lord loveth a cheerful giver,' and I knew

I could give the penny a lot more cheerfully than I could give the quarter, so I gave it."

A minister asked a little girl what she thought of her first church service.

"The music was nice," she said, "but the commercial was too long."

A couple was touring the capitol in Washington D.C., and the guide pointed out a tall, benevolent gentleman as the congressional chaplain.

The lady asked, "What does the chaplain do? Does he pray for the Senate or House?"

The guide answered, "No, he gets up, looks at the Congress, then prays for the country!"

Three sons of a lawyer, a doctor, and a minister were talking about how much money their fathers made.

The lawyer's son said, "My father goes into court on a case and often comes home with as much as $1500."

The doctor's son said, "My father performs an operation and earns as much as $2000."

The minister's son, determined not to be outdone, said, "That's nothing. My father preaches for just 20 minutes on Sunday morning and it takes four men to carry the money."

The new preacher, at his first service, had a pitcher of water and a glass on the pulpit. As he preached, he drank until the pitcher of water was completely gone.

After the service someone asked an old woman of the church, "How did you like the new pastor?"

"Fine," she said, "but he's the first windmill I ever saw that was run by water."

After a long, dry sermon, the minister announced that he wished to meet with the church board following the close of the service. The first man to arrive was a stranger. "You misunderstood my announcement. This is a meeting of the board," said the minister.

"I know," said the man, "but if there is anyone here more bored than I am, I'd like to meet him."

There was a certain energetic young preacher who had a thriving country church. He was always prodding his people to do greater things for God, and he spent much time in preparation of his sermons.

There was a deacon in his congregation who did little and seemed to care less. It caused the young preacher much concern. On several occasions the preacher would tell him exactly what he thought. The old deacon never caught the point. The old deacon always thought he was referring to someone else. One Sunday, the preacher made it plainer as to whom he was talking. Following the service the deacon said, "Preacher, you sure told them today."

The next sermon was still more pointed than ever.

Again the deacon said, "Preacher, you sure told them today."

The next Sunday it rained so hard that no one was at the church except this one deacon. The preacher thought that he would now know about whom he was talking. The sermon went straight to the deacon who was the only one in the congregation. Following the service, the deacon walked up to the preacher and said, "Preacher, you sure told them if they had been here."

A Sunday school teacher asked Little Willie who the first man in the Bible was.

48

"Hoss," said Willie.

"No," said the teacher. "It was Adam."

"Ah, shucks!" Willie replied. "I knew it was one of those Cartwrights."

My son is such an introvert he can't even lead in silent prayer.

A minister forgot the name of a couple he was going to marry so he said from the pulpit, "Will those wishing to be united in holy matrimony please come forward after the service."

After the service 13 old maids came forward.

A new preacher had just begun his sermon. He was a little nervous and about ten minutes into the talk his mind went blank. He remembered what they had taught him in seminary when a situation like this would arise—repeat your last point. Often this would help you remember what is coming next. So he thought he would give it a try.

"Behold, I come quickly," he said. Still his mind was blank. He thought he would try it again. "Behold, I come quickly." Still nothing.

He tried it one more time with such force he fell forward, knocking the pulpit to one side, tripping over a flowerpot and falling into the lap of a little old lady in the front row.

The young preacher apologized and tried to explain what happened.

"That's all right, young man," said the lady. "It was my fault. I should have gotten out of the way. You told me three times you were coming!"

Old Pete was very close to dying but made a miraculous recovery. In the hospital his pastor came to visit him.

"Tell me, Pete, when you were so near death's door, were you afraid to meet your Maker?"

"No, Pastor," said Pete. "It was the other man I was afraid of!"

A Sunday school teacher asked her students to draw a picture of Jesus' family. After the pictures were brought to her, she saw that some of the youngsters had drawn the conventional pictures—the family and the manger, the family riding on the mule, and so on.

But she called up one little boy to ask him to explain his drawing, which showed an airplane with four heads sticking out of the windows.

She said, "I can understand you drew three of the heads to show Joseph, Mary, and Jesus. But who's the fourth head?"

"Oh," answered the boy, "that's Pontius the pilot!"

Pastor: Isn't this a beautiful church? And here's a plaque for the men who died in the service.
Man: Which one . . . morning or evening?

One friend to another: "You drive the car and I'll pray."
"What's the matter? Don't you trust my driving?"
"Don't you trust my praying?"

Member: Pastor, how did you get that cut on your face?
Pastor: I was thinking about my sermon this morning and wasn't concentrating on what I was doing so I cut myself while shaving.
Member: That's too bad! Next time you'd better concentrate on your shaving and cut your sermon!

A parishioner had dozed off during the morning service.
"Will all who want to go to heaven stand?" the preacher asked.
All stood except the sleeping parishioner.

After they sat down, the pastor continued: "Well, will all who want to go to the other place stand?"

Someone suddenly dropped a songbook and the sleeping man jumped to his feet and stood sheepishly facing the preacher. He mumbled confusedly, "Well, preacher, I don't know what we're voting for, but it looks like you and I are the only ones for it."

Right in the middle of the service, just before the sermon, one of the congregation remembered she had forgotten to turn off the gas under the roast. Hurriedly she scribbled a note and passed it to the usher to give to her husband. Unfortunately, the usher misunderstood her intention and took it to the pulpit. Unfolding the note, the preacher read aloud, "Please go home and turn off the gas."

A little boy forgot his lines in a Sunday school presentation. His mother, sitting in the front row to prompt him, gestured and formed the words silently with her lips, but it didn't help. Her son's memory was blank.

Finally she leaned forward and whispered the cue, "I am the light of the world."

The child beamed and with great feeling and a loud, clear voice said, "My mother is the light of the world."

Clara: My pastor is so good he can talk on any subject for an hour.
Sarah: That's nothing! My pastor can talk for an hour without a subject!

Preacher: Please take it easy on the bill for repairing my car. Remember, I am a poor preacher.
Mechanic: I know; I heard you Sunday!

Two men were bosom buddies. Much to the amazement of one, the other became a Sunday school teacher.

"I bet you don't even know the Lord's Prayer," the other man fumed.

"Everybody knows that," the other replied. "It's 'Now I lay me down to sleep. . .'"

"You win," said the other admiringly. "I didn't know you knew so much about the Bible."

Member: How are you feeling, pastor?
Pastor: Better.

Member: We had a committee meeting the other night, and they voted to send you this get-well card. The motion passed 4 to 3!

A Sunday school teacher asked a little girl if she said her prayers every night.

"No, not every night," declared the child. "'Cause some nights I don't want anything!"

The chaplain was passing through the prison garment factory. "Sewing?" he asked a prisoner who was at work.

"No, chaplain," replied the prisoner gloomily, "reaping!"

Correcting Sunday school lessons one day, a teacher found that little Jimmy had written: "Harold be Thy name" as well as "Give us this day our jelly bread."

A Sunday school teacher asked her class to draw a picture illustrating a Bible story. One paper handed in contained a picture of a big car. An old man with long whiskers flying in the breeze was driving. A man and a woman were seated in the backseat. Puzzled, the teacher asked little Jimmy to explain his drawing. "Why, that is God. He's driving Adam and Eve out of the Garden of Eden."

A hungry little boy was beginning to eat his dinner when his father reminded him that they hadn't prayed.

"We don't have to," said the little boy. "Mommy is a good cook!"

Little Mary, the daughter of a radio announcer, was invited to a friend's house for dinner. The hostess asked if Mary would honor them by saying grace.

Delighted, the little girl cleared her throat, looked at her wristwatch, and said, "This good food, friends, is coming to you through the courtesy of Almighty God!"

On the way home from church a little boy asked his mother, "Is it true, Mommy, that we are made of dust?"

"Yes, darling."

"And do we go back to dust again when we die?"

"Yes, dear."

"Well, Mommy, when I said my prayers last night and looked under the bed, I found someone who is either coming or going."

One Sunday a farmer went to church. When he entered he saw that he and the preacher were the only ones present. The preacher asked the farmer if he wanted him to go ahead and preach. The farmer said, "I'm not too smart, but if I went to feed my cattle and only one showed up, I'd feed him." So the minister began his sermon.

One hour passed, then two hours, then two-and-a-half hours. The preacher finally finished and came down to ask the farmer how he had liked the sermon.

The farmer answered slowly, "Well, I'm not very smart, but if I went to feed my cattle and only one showed up, I sure wouldn't feed him all the hay."

Little Susie concluded her prayer by saying: "Dear God, before I finish, please take care of Daddy, take care of Mommy, take care of my baby brother, Grandma, and Grandpa . . . and please, God, take care of yourself—or else we're all sunk!"

A Sunday school teacher asked her class to write a composition on the story of Samson. One teenage girl wrote, "Samson wasn't so unusual. The boys I know brag about their strength and wear their hair long too."

The teacher handed out the test papers and told the children they could start answering the questions.

She noticed little Billy sitting with his head bowed, his hands over his face. She approached him.

"Don't you feel well?" she inquired.

"Oh, I'm fine, teacher. I always pray before a test!"

A minister was about to baptize a baby. Turning to the father, he inquired, "His name, please?"

"William Patrick Arthur Timothy John MacArthur."

The minister turned to his assistant and said, "A little more water, please."

❖ ❖ ❖

A little boy excited about his part in the Christmas play came home and said, "I got a part in the Christmas play!"

"What part?" asked his mother.

"I'm one of the three wise guys!" was the reply.

St. Peter looked at the new arrival skeptically; he'd had no advance knowledge of his coming.

"How did you get here?" he asked.

"Flu."

The boys were trying to outdo each other. The first said, "My uncle's a doctor. I can be sick for nothing!" The second youngster shot back, "Big deal! My uncle is a preacher. I can be good for nothing!"

"Mommy," asked little Judy, "did you ever see a cross-eyed bear?"

"Why, no, Judy," chuckled her mother. "Why do you ask?"

"Well, in Sunday school this morning, we sang about 'the consecrated cross-eyed bear.' "

The sermon was very long this Sunday morning and Donny was getting more restless by the minute.

Suddenly, in a whisper too loud for his mother's comfort, he blurted out, "If we give him the money now, Ma, will he let us go?"

"Daddy, I want to ask you a question," said Bobby after his first day in Sunday school.

"Yes, Bobby, what is it?"

"The teacher was reading the Bible to us—all about the children of Israel building the temple, the children of Israel crossing the Red Sea, the children of Israel making sacrifices. Didn't the grown-ups do anything?"

The young girl of the house, by way of punishment for some minor misdemeanor, was compelled to eat her dinner alone at a little table in a corner of the dining room. The rest of the family paid no attention to her presence until they heard her audibly praying over her repast: "I thank thee, Lord, for preparing a table before me in the presence of mine enemies."

People who cough incessantly never seem to go to a doctor—they go to banquets, concerts, and church.

❖ ❖ ❖

Did you hear about the man from the income tax bureau who phoned a certain minister and said, "We're checking the tax return of a member of your church, and we noticed he listed a donation to your building fund of $300. Is that correct?"

The minister answered without hesitation, "I haven't got my records available, but I'll promise you one thing: If he hasn't he will!"

The minister's daughter was sent to bed with a stomachache and missed her usual romp with her daddy. A few minutes later she appeared at the top of the stairs and called to her mother, "Mama, let me talk with Daddy."

"No, my dear, not tonight. Get back in bed."

"Please, Mama."

"I said 'no.' That's enough now."

"Mother, I'm a very sick woman, and I must see my pastor at once."

Crusty Characters

His trouble is too much bone in the head and not enough in the back.

He has a concrete mind . . . permanently set and all mixed up.

He's a man of rare intelligence . . . it's rare when he shows any.

You know, if brains were dynamite, she wouldn't have enough to blow her nose!

He's just as smart as he can be . . . unfortunately.

She has a keen sense of rumor.

You could make a fortune if you could buy him for what you think of him and sell him for what he thinks of himself.

He's a second-story man; no one ever believes his first story.

When she meets another egotist, it's an I for an I.

He's always down on everything he's not up on.

He doesn't want anyone to make a fuss over him . . . just to treat him as they would any other great man.

Be careful when you're speaking about him . . . you're speaking of the man he loves.

Someone should push the "down" button on her elevator shoes.

She says that whenever she's down in the dumps she gets a new hat. I've always thought that's where she gets them.

He has a great labor-saving device . . . tomorrow.

He's a regular "Rock of Jello."

She is so nervous that she keeps coffee awake.

He's the real decisive type . . . he'll give you a definite "maybe."

They call her "Jigsaw." Every time she's faced with a problem she goes to pieces.

He left his job because of illness and fatigue. His boss got sick and tired of him.

The only thing she's ever achieved on her own is dandruff.

Some cause happiness wherever they go; others whenever they go.

He had to see the doctor in the morning for a blood test, so he stayed up all night studying for it.

She has delusions of glamour!

He's one person who would make a perfect stranger!

She made him a millionaire. Before she married him, he was a billionaire.

He can stay longer in an hour than most people do in a week.

When it comes to telling her age, she's shy . . . about ten years shy.

There's no doubt he's trying. In fact, he's very trying.

He stopped drinking coffee in the morning because it keeps him awake the rest of the day.

11

Do You Know?

How do you milk an ant?
First, you get a low stool . . .

What's more clever than speaking in several
languages?
Keeping your mouth shut in one.

How do you tune "hard rock" instruments?
You don't.

What kind of fish do you eat with peanut
butter?
Jellyfish.

When rain falls, does it ever get up again?
Yes, in dew time.

What do you get when you cross a porcupine
  with a sheep?
An animal that knits its own sweaters.

What happens when two bullets get married?
They have a little BB.

What does the government use when it takes a
  census of all the monkeys in Africa?
An ape recorder.

What do you get if you cross a chicken with an
  elephant?
*I don't know, but Colonel Sanders would have a lot of
  trouble trying to dip it into the batter.*

If a dog lost his tail, where would he get another
  one?
At the retail store, naturally.

Why does the ocean roar?
You would too if you had lobsters in your bed.

What has four legs and flies?
A picnic table.

What is the definition of a financial genius?
A person who can earn money faster than the family can spend it.

What is another name for toupee?
Top secret.

Why did Humpty Dumpty have a great fall?
To make up for a terrible summer.

What's worse than a giraffe with a sore throat?
A hippopotamus with chapped lips.

What do they call a man who still has his tonsils and appendix?
A doctor.

How do you get rid of company that stays
too long?
Treat them like family.

What is the longest word in the English
language?
*Smiles—because there's a mile between the first
and last letter.*

What is the best way to keep fish from smelling?
Cut off their noses.

What is more blessed to give than receive?
Advice.

What do you call a person who crosses the ocean
twice without taking a bath?
A dirty double crosser.

What animal has the smallest appetite?
A moth. It just eat holes.

What book contains more stirring pages than
any other book?
A cookbook.

Why should you always take a watch with you
when you cross the desert?
Because there is a spring in it.

What is black and white and red all over?
A zebra with a sunburn.

What do you call a camel without a hump?
Humphrey.

What two words have the most letters?
Post office.

If a man smashed a clock, could he be convicted
of killing time?
Not if he could prove that the clock struck first.

What did the leftovers say when they were put
into the freezer?
Foiled again.

Where do jellyfish get their jelly?
From ocean currents.

Is it difficult to eat soup with a mustache?
Yes, it is quite a strain.

What is another name for a nursery?
Bawlroom.

What do you call a monkey that sells potato
chips?
A chipmonk.

In what month do people talk the least?
February.

What do you get when you cross an elephant
with a computer?
A 5,000-pound know-it-all.

Why do people laugh up their sleeves?
Because that's where their funny bones are.

What is the name of a tourniquet worn on the
left hand to stop circulation?
An engagement ring.

How can you jump off a 50-foot ladder and not
get hurt?
Jump off the first rung.

What machine scares the daylights into you?
An alarm clock.

What's the difference between a mental institution and a college?
*In the mental institution you must show improve-
ment to get out.*

If you have seven apples and I ask you for two,
    how many would you have left?
Seven.

What is another name for a juvenile delinquent?
Child hood.

What is the difference between unlawful and
    illegal?
An illegal is a sick bird.

If all the people in the United States owned pink
    cars, what would the country be called?
A pink carnation.

12

Education

A wise schoolteacher sends this note to all parents on the first day of school: "If you promise not to believe everything your child says happens at school, I'll promise not to believe everything he or she says happens at home."

Teacher: What are you—animal, vegetable, or mineral?
Little boy: Vegetable. I'm a human bean!

Tony: My college has turned out some great men.
Daisy: I didn't know you were a college graduate.
Tony: I'm one they turned out!

It was the little girl's first day at school, and the teacher was making out her registration card.

"What is your father's name?" she asked.

"Daddy," replied the child.

"Yes, I know, but what does your mother call him?"

"Oh, she doesn't call him anything. She likes him!"

Teacher: Why don't you brush your teeth? I can see what you had for breakfast this morning.
Student: What did I have?
Teacher: Eggs!
Student: You're wrong! That was yesterday!

Girl: Too bad you flunked the test. How far were you from the right answer?
Boy: Two seats!

❖ ❖ ❖

A young college student had stayed up all night studying for his zoology test the next day. As he entered the classroom, he saw ten stands with ten birds on them. Each bird had a sack over its head; only the legs were showing. He sat right in the front row because he wanted to do the best job possible. The professor announced that the test would be to look at each of the birds' legs and give the common name, habitat, genus, and species.

The student looked at each of the birds' legs. They all looked the same to him. He began to get upset. He had stayed up all night studying and now had to identify birds by their legs. The more he thought about it the madder he got.

Finally he could stand it no longer. He went up to the professor's desk and said, "What a stupid test! How could anyone tell the difference between birds by looking at their legs?" With that the student threw his test on the professor's desk and walked to the door.

The professor was surprised. The class was so big that he didn't know every student's name so as the student reached the door the professor called, "Mister, what's your name?"

The enraged student pulled up his pant legs and said, "You tell me, buddy! You tell me!"

A father was examining his son's report card. "One thing is definitely in your favor," he announced. "With this report card, you couldn't possibly be cheating."

There's one great thing to be said for a college education. It enables you to worry about things all over the world.

A college student with coin in hand said: "If it's heads, I go to bed. If it's tails, I stay up. If it stands on edge, I study."

Professor: If there are any dumbbells in the room, please stand up.

There was a long pause, then a lone freshman stood up in the rear.

Professor: What? Do you consider yourself a dumbbell?

Freshman: Well, not exactly, but I hate to see you standing all alone.

Teacher: Johnny, give me a sentence with a direct object.

Johnny: Teacher, everybody thinks you're beautiful.

Teacher: Thank you, Johnny, but what is the object?

Johnny: A good report card.

Teacher: If your mother gave you a large apple
and a small one, then told you to share with
your brother, which one would you give him?

Johnnie: Do you mean my little brother or my
big brother?

For weeks a six-year-old lad kept telling his
first-grade teacher about the baby brother or sister that was expected at his house. Then one day
the mother allowed the boy to feel the move-
ments of the unborn child. The six-year-old was
obviously impressed, but made no comment.
Furthermore, he stopped telling his teacher
about the impending event.

The teacher finally sat down with the boy
and said, "Tommy, whatever has become of that
baby brother or sister you were expecting at
home?"

Tommy burst into tears and confessed, "I
think Mommy ate it!"

Librarian: Please be quiet. The people next to
you can't read.

Girl: What a shame! I've been reading since I
was six.

Teacher: Billy, what did you do when Ed called you a liar?

Billy: I remembered what you told me: "A soft answer turns away anger."

Teacher: Very good, Billy. What answer did you give him?

Billy: I answered him with a soft tomato.

Teacher: Really, Tommy, your handwriting is terrible! You must learn to write better.

Tommy: Well, if I did, you'd be finding fault with my spelling.

Teacher: What is an emperor?

Georgia: I don't know.

Teacher: An emperor is a ruler.

Georgia: Oh, sure. I used to carry an emperor to school with me.

✧ ✧ ✧

"Some plants," said the teacher, "have the prefix 'dog.' For instance, there is the dogrose, the dogwood, and the dogviolet. Who can name another plant prefixed by 'dog'?"

"I can," shouted a little boy in the back row. "Collieflower."

As a special treat, a teacher took her class to visit a museum of natural history. The children returned home excitedly. On rushing into his house, one of the little boys greeted his mother exuberantly: "What do you think we did today, Mother? The teacher took us to a dead circus!"

Interrupted by the sound of the bell announcing the end of the class, the professor was annoyed to see the students noisily preparing to leave although he was in the middle of his lecture. "Just a moment, gentlemen," he said, "I have a few more pearls to cast."

Teacher: Johnny, how much is three times three.
Johnny: Nine.
Teacher: That's pretty good.
Johnny: Pretty good? Say, "It's perfect.'"

He was in school so long the other pupils used to bring him apples thinking he was the teacher.

Sometimes you wonder what kids are really learning. Yesterday a teacher pointed at the flag, turned to my six-year-old, and asked him what it was.

He answered, "It is the flag of my country!"

The teacher couldn't leave well enough alone. She said, "Now tell me the name of the country."

And he said, " 'Tis of thee!' "

Teacher: I hope I didn't see you looking at someone else's paper, Billy.
Billy: I hope so, too, Teacher.

Student: I don't think I deserve a zero on this test!
Teacher: Neither do I, but it's the lowest mark I can give you.

A college boy to his mother: "I decided that I want to be a political science major, and I want to clean up the mess in the world!"

"That's very nice," purred his mother. "You can go upstairs and start with your room."

A student wrote the following on his pre-Christmas examination paper: "God only knows the answer to this question. Merry Christmas!"

The professor returned the paper with the following notation: "God gets an 'A'; you get an 'F.' Happy New Year."

Teacher: Where's your homework this morning?
Student: You'll never believe this, but on the way to school I made a paper airplane out of it and someone hijacked it to Cuba!

Teacher: What do you call a person who keeps on talking when people are no longer interested?
Student: A teacher.

Teacher: What's the formula for water?
Student: H,I,J,K,L,M,N,O.
Teacher: That's not the formula I gave you.
Student: Yes, it is. You said it was H to O.

◇13◇

Family Frolic

Girl: The man I marry must stand out in
    company, be musical, tell jokes, line dance,
    and stay at home nights.
Mother: You don't want a husband—you want
    a TV set.

Father pacing the floor with a wailing baby
in his arms as his wife lies snug in bed: "No one
ever asks me how I manage to combine mar-
riage and a career."

My children are at the perfect age . . . too
old to cry at night and too young to borrow my
car.

When the father called home, the six-year-old son answered and said, "Don't talk too loud, Dad, the babysitter is asleep."

Friend: How is your new "doctor" son getting along in his practice?
Mother: Fine. He is doing so well he can occasionally tell a patient there is nothing the matter with him.

Father: Why don't you get a job?
Son: Why?
Father: So you can earn some money.
Son: Why?
Father: So you can put some money in a bank account and earn interest.
Son: Why?
Father: So that when you're old you can use the money in your bank account and never have to work again.
Son: But, I'm not working now!

Son: Here's my report card, Dad, along with one of your old ones I found in the attic.

Father: Well, son, you're right. This old report card of mine you found isn't any better than yours. I guess the only fair thing to do is give you what my father gave me.

Son: Dad, what is "creeping inflation"?
Father: It's when your mother starts out asking for new shoes and ends up with a complete new outfit.

The best way for a stay-at-home mom to get a few minutes to herself at the end of the day is to start doing the dishes.

Father: Do you think it will improve Junior's behavior if we buy him a bicycle?
Mother: No, but it'll spread it over a wider area.

Mother to fussy son: Twenty years from now you'll be telling some girl what a great cook your mother was . . . now eat your dinner.

Father to teenage son: Do you mind if I use the car tonight? I'm taking your mother out and I want to impress her.

Mother: Every time you're naughty I get another
    gray hair.
Son: Gee, Mom, you must have been a terror
    when you were young . . . just look at
    Grandma.

Son: Dad, will you help me find the least com-
    mon denominator in this math problem?
Dad: Don't tell me that hasn't been found—they
    were looking for it when I was a kid.

❖ ❖ ❖

Photographer (to young man): It will make a
    much better picture if you put your hand on
    your father's shoulder.
Father: It would be much more natural if he had
    his hand in my pocket.

Two cub scouts whose younger brother had
fallen into a shallow pond rushed home to
Mother with tears in their eyes. "We're trying to
give him artificial respiration," one of them
sobbed, "but he keeps getting up and walking
away."

Mother: Donna, you shouldn't always keep
    everything for yourself. I've told you before
    that you should let your little brother play
    with your toys half of the time.
Donna: I've been doing that. I take the sled
    going downhill, and he takes it going up.

In a country home that seldom had guests,
the young son was eager to help his mother after
his father appeared with two dinner guests from
the office.

When the dinner was nearly over, the boy
went to the kitchen and proudly carried in the
first piece of apple pie, giving it to his father,
who passed it to a guest.

The boy came in with a second piece of pie
and gave it to his father, who again gave it to a
guest.

This was too much for the boy, who said,
"It's no use, Dad. The pieces are all the same
size."

Little Billy was left to fix lunch. When his
mother returned with a friend, she noticed that
Billy had already strained the tea.

"Did you find the tea strainer?" his mother
asked.

"No, mother, I couldn't, so I used the fly swatter," replied Billy.

His mother nearly fainted, so Billy hastily added, "Don't get excited, Mother. I used an old one."

The 12-year-old boy stood patiently beside the clock counter while the store clerk waited on all of the adult customers. Finally he got around to the youngster, who made his purchase and hurried out to the curb, where his father was impatiently waiting in his car.

"What took you so long, son?" he asked.

"The man waited on everybody in the store before me," the boy replied. "But I got even."

"How?"

"I wound and set all the alarm clocks while I was waiting," the youngster explained happily. "It's going to be a mighty noisy place at eight o'clock."

Mother: Were you a good boy in school today?
Son: How much trouble can you get into standing in a corner all day?

"Did you see how pleased Mrs. Smith looked when I told her she didn't look a day older than her daughter?"

"I didn't notice Mrs. Smith. . . . I was too busy watching the expression on the daughter's face!"

First man: I keep a gun handy in case anyone breaks into my house.

Second man: If a burglar came into our bedroom during the night, I'd get up and take him to the bathroom.

❖ ❖ ❖

"Young man," said the angry father from the head of the stairs, "didn't I hear the clock strike four when you brought my daughter in?"

"You did," admitted the boyfriend. "It was going to strike eleven, but I grabbed it and held the gong so it wouldn't disturb you."

The father muttered, "Doggone! Why didn't I think of that one in my courting days!"

14

Famous Last Words

"You can make it easy . . . that train isn't coming fast."

✧ ✧ ✧

"Gimme a match. I think my gas tank is empty."

✧ ✧ ✧

"Wife, these biscuits are tough."

✧ ✧ ✧

"Step on her, boy, we're only going 75."

✧ ✧ ✧

"Just watch me dive from that bridge."

✧ ✧ ✧

"If you knew anything you wouldn't be a traffic cop."

"What? Your mother is going to stay another month?"

"Say, who's boss of this joint, anyhow?"

15

Food

A man walked into a restaurant in a strange town. The waiter came and asked him for his order. Feeling lonely, he replied, "Meat loaf and a kind word." When the waiter returned with the meat loaf, the man said, "Where's the good word?"

The waiter put down the meat loaf and sighed, bent down, and whispered, "Don't eat the meat loaf."

Cook: Do you want me to cut this pizza into six or eight pieces?

Man: You'd better make it six. . . . I don't think I can eat eight pieces!

Customer: Do you serve crabs in this dump?
Waiter: Yes, sir. What'll you have?

"Waiter!" shouted an irate customer. "I can't tell whether this is coffee or tea! It tastes like gasoline!"

"If it tastes like gasoline then it positively is coffee," the waiter said. "Our tea tastes like turpentine."

"Waiter," said the surprised customer as he examined his check, "What's this eight dollars for?"

"For the chopped liver sandwich, sir."

"Yeah?" The customer nodded. "Whose liver was it—the president's?"

✧ ✧ ✧

The manager of a restaurant called his waitresses together. "Women," he began, "I want you to all look your best today. Greet every customer with a smile and a kind word."

"What's up?" asked one of the women. "Bunch of big shots coming in today?"

"No, the meat's tough today."

Customer: Those franks you sold me were meat at one end and cornmeal at the other!
Butcher: Yes, ma'am. In these times it's difficult to make both ends meat.

Man: I can't eat this food! Call the manager!
Waitress: It's no use, sir. He can't eat it either.

A meek little man in a restaurant timidly touched the arm of a man putting on an overcoat. "Excuse me," he said, "but do you happen to be Mr. Smith of Newport?"

"No, I'm not!" the man answered impatiently.

"Oh—er—well," stammered the first man, "you see, I am, and that's his overcoat you're putting on."

Sign in a restaurant: Our customers are always right: misinformed, perhaps, inexact, bullheaded, fickle, even downright stupid, but never wrong.

Joe: A panhandler came up to me and said he
hadn't had a bite in two weeks.
Moe: Poor fellow. What did you do?
Joe: Bit him of course!

I know a woman who has cooked so many
TV dinners she thinks she's in show business.

✧ ✧ ✧

Man: Do you serve breakfast here?
Waitress: Sure; what'll it be?
Man: Let me have watery scrambled eggs . . .
some burnt toast . . . and some weak coffee,
lukewarm.
Waitress: Whatever you say, sir.
Man: Now, are you doing anything while that
order is going through?
Waitress: Why—no, sir.
Man: Then sit here and nag me awhile. . . . I'm
homesick!

I hate to always eat and run, but the way I
tip it's the only safe procedure.

❖ ❖ ❖

Customer: Your sign says, "$50 to anyone who orders something we can't furnish." I would like to have an elephant ear sandwich.
Waiter: Ohhh . . . we're going to have to pay you the $50.
Customer: No elephant ears, huh?
Waiter: Oh, we've got lots of them . . . but we're all out of those big buns!

"A fellow walked up to me today and asked for a dollar for a cup of coffee. I gave it to him, and then followed him clear across town to the restaurant."

Customer: What flavors of ice cream do you have?
Hoarse waiter: Vanilla, strawberry, and chocolate.
Customer: Do you have laryngitis?
Waiter: No, just vanilla, strawberry, and chocolate.

Shopper: The way food prices are going up, it soon will be cheaper to eat the money.

Diner: What would you recommend for tonight?
Waiter: Go someplace else . . . the cook is on
strike.

Percy: I won't criticize their chef, but you'll
notice three shakers on every table . . . salt,
pepper, and Alka-Seltzer.

Waiter: Would you like your coffee black?
Customer: What other colors do you have?

Diner: What's this fly doing in my soup?
Waiter: The backstroke.

Customer: Waitress, why is my doughnut all
smashed?
Waitress: You said you wanted a cup of coffee
and a doughnut, and step on it.

Waiter: And how did you find your steak, sir?
Customer: I just lifted one of the brussels
sprouts and there it was!

Customer: This food isn't fit for a pig!
Waiter: I'm sorry, sir. I'll bring you some that is.

Tim: Look, Jim, why are you always trying to
    impress me? So you spoke to the waiter in
    French! So, big deal! So what good is it to
    know French? . . .What did he tell you,
    waiter?
Waiter: He told me to give you the check, sir!

Customer: Your sign says, "Any sandwich you
    can name." I would like a whale sandwich.
Waiter: Okay. (He disappears into the kitchen
    and shortly returns.) I'm afraid I can't get you
    a whale sandwich.
Customer: Why not? . . .your sign says "any
    sandwich."
Waiter: The cook says he doesn't want to start a
    new whale for one lousy sandwich.

16

Getting Older

Middle age is when you know all the answers and nobody asks you the questions.

Three states of man: youth, middle age, "you're looking fine!"

There are three ways to tell if you are getting old: first, a loss of memory; second . . .

The hardest decision in life is when to start middle age.

Middle age is when the narrow waist and the broad mind begin to change places.

Golf

Bill: I'd move heaven and earth to break my 100 score.

Phil: Try moving heaven. You've already moved plenty of earth today.

Caddy: Let me say this about your game, mister. I wouldn't say you were the worst golfer I have seen on this course, but I've seen places today that I've never seen before.

"Look," the golfer screamed at his caddy, "if you don't keep your big mouth shut, you'll drive me out of my mind."

"That's no drive, mister," corrected the caddy. "That's a putt."

Golfer: Notice any improvement since last year?
Caddy: Polished your clubs, didn't you?

Golfer: Why do you keep looking at your watch?
Caddy: This isn't a watch, sir. It's a compass.

Golfer: The doctor says I can't play golf.
Caddy: Oh, he's played with you, too, huh?

"Caddy, why didn't you see where that ball went?"

"Well, it doesn't usually go anywhere, Mrs. Smith. You caught me off-guard."

The other day I was playing golf and saw an unusual thing. A golfer became so mad that he threw his brand-new set of golf clubs into the lake. A few minutes later he came back, waded into the lake, and retrieved his clubs. He proceeded to take his car keys out of the bag—then threw the clubs back into the water.

Golfer: Well, what do you think of my game?
Caddy: I guess it's all right, but I still like golf
better.

Golfer: How would you have played that last
shot, caddy?
Caddy: Under an assumed name!

Golfer: You must be the world's worst caddy!
Caddy: No, sir! That would be too much of a
coincidence!

Hot Air

A speaker was having a little trouble getting started in his speech. All of the sudden someone from the audience shouted: "Tell 'em all you know. It will only take a minute."

"I'll tell 'em all we both know," shot back the speaker. "It won't take any longer."

A manufacturer of bicycle tires was the speaker at a business luncheon. In response to a toast, he said: "I have no desire or intention to inflict upon you a long speech for it is well known in our trade that the longer the spoke, the bigger the tire."

Once during a debate Abraham Lincoln was accused by Stephen Douglas of being two-faced.

Without hesitation Lincoln calmly replied, "I leave it to my audience . . . if I had two faces, would I be wearing this one?"

"That was a great speech, sir. I like the straightforward way you dodged those issues."

At a lecture series a very poor speaker was on the platform. As he was speaking, people in the audience began to get up and leave. After about ten minutes there was only one man left. Finally the man stopped speaking and asked the man why he remained to the end.

"I'm the next speaker," was the reply.

A lecturer announced to his audience that the world would probably end in seven billion years.

"How long did you say?" came a terrified voice from the rear.

"Seven billion years."

"Thank goodness!" said the voice. "I thought for a moment you said seven million."

19

It's All in
the Family

Advice to mothers: Unless you deliberately set aside a little time for regular relaxation, you will not be able to efficiently care for your family. Therefore, plan to relax a minimum of an hour-and-a-half every 15 years.

One day Johnny's father brought his boss home for dinner. When Johnny's mother served the meat, the little boy asked, "Is this mutton?"

The mother replied, "No. Why do you ask?"

"Because Dad said he was going to bring home a muttonhead for dinner," Johnny answered.

Adolescence is a period of rapid changes. Between the ages of 12 and 17, for example, a child may see his parents age 20 years.

After dinner, members of a lot of families suffer from dishtemper.

Father: What's wrong, Judy? Usually you talk on the phone for hours. This time you only talked half an hour. How come?
Judy: It was a wrong number.

A father, whose looks aren't anything to brag about, tells this on himself:

My little girl was sitting on my lap facing a mirror. After gazing intently at her reflection for some minutes, she said, "Daddy, did God make you?"

"Certainly, my dear," I told her.

"And did He make me, too?" she asked, taking another look in the mirror.

"Certainly, dear. What makes you ask?"

"Seems to me He's doing better work lately."

A letter from a college student said, "Please send food packages! All they serve here is breakfast, lunch, and dinner."

Mother: Aunt Mathilda won't kiss you with that
    dirty face.
Boy: That's what I figured.

"Dear Dad: Let me hear from you more
often, even if it's only a five or ten."

"In our family," a little girl told her teacher,
"everybody marries relatives. My father married
my mother, my uncle married my aunt, and the
other day I found out that my grandmother married my grandfather."

Father: Well, son, what did you learn in school
    today?
Son: I learned to say, "Yes, sir," and "No, sir,"
    and "Yes, ma'am," and "No, ma'am."
Father: Really?
Son: Yeah!

Nowadays you'll find almost everything in
the average American home . . . except the family.

Father of teenage son to neighbor: Junior's at
that awkward age . . . too old for a spanking
and too young for analysis.

Son: Dad, the Bible says if you don't let me have
the car, you hate me.
Father: Where does it say that?
Son: Proverbs 13:24—"He that spareth the rod
hateth his son."

Husband: It must be time to get up.
Wife: How can you tell?
Husband: The baby has fallen asleep at last.

Coed: Daddy, the girl who sits next to me in
class has a dress just like mine.
Dad: So you want a new dress?
Coed: Well, it would be cheaper than changing
colleges.

Jed: Your sister is spoiled, isn't she?
Ted: No, that's the perfume she uses.

Billy was in a store with his mother when he was given a stick of candy by one of the clerks.

"What do you say, Billy?" prompted his mother.

"Charge it!" he replied.

The mother said firmly, "If you two boys can't agree and be quiet, I shall take your pie away."

The younger one replied, "But, Mother, we do agree. Bill wants the biggest piece, and so do I!"

Mother: Eat your spinach. It will put color in your cheeks.

Son: Who wants green cheeks?

❖ ❖ ❖

There was an earthquake recently that frightened the inhabitants of a certain town. One couple sent their little boy to stay with an uncle in another district, explaining the reason for the nephew's sudden visit. A day later the parents received this telegram, "Am returning your boy. Send the earthquake."

Johnny: Will I get everything I pray for, Mama?
Mother: Everything that's good for you, dear.
Johnny: Oh, what's the use, then? I get that
    anyway.

"Mother, do give me another piece of sugar,"
little Helen requested.

"But you've had three already," her mother
pointed out.

"Just one more, please."

"Well, this must be the last."

"Thank you, Mother . . . but I must say, you
have no willpower."

Auntie: When I was a child, I was told if I made
    ugly faces I would stay like that.
Little Joan: Well, you can't say you weren't
    warned, Auntie.

Little boy to departing relative: There's no hurry,
    Uncle. Daddy has put the clock a whole hour
    ahead.

✧ ✧ ✧

Bobby had been to a birthday party, and, knowing his weakness, his mother looked him straight in the eyes and said, "I hope you didn't ask for a second piece of cake."

"No," replied Bobby. "I only asked Mrs. Jones for the recipe so you could make some like it, and she gave me two more pieces of her own accord."

Little boy (calling father at office): Hello, who is this?

Father (recognizing son's voice): The smartest man in the world.

Little boy: Pardon me; I must have the wrong number.

Father: Can you support her in the way she's accustomed to?

Prospective son-in-law: No, I can't support her in the manner she has been accustomed to, but I can support her in the way her mother was accustomed to when she was first married.

Son: Dad, what is a weapon?
Father: Why, son, that's something you fight with.
Son: Is mother your weapon?

A little boy never said a word for six years. One day his parents served him cocoa. From out of left field the kid says, "This cocoa's no good." His parents went around raving. They said to him, "Why did you wait so long to talk?" He said, "Up till now everything's been okay."

Father: Don't you think our son gets all his brains from me?
Mother: Probably. I still have all mine.

Parents spend the first part of a child's life urging him to walk and talk, and the rest of his childhood making him sit down and keep quiet.

Harv
by

For more information about Bob Phillips' books,
send a self-addressed stamped envelope to:

Family Services
P.O. Box 9363
Fresno, California 93702